Free Pre-College Programs
A Guide to No-Cost and Low-Cost Summer Programs for Teens

FREE PRE-COLLEGE PROGRAMS

A Guide to No-Cost and Low-Cost Summer Programs for Teens

By Lynnette Khalfani Cox

Advantage World Press

Published by Advantage World Press
An Imprint of TheMoneyCoach.net, LLC
P.O. Box 1307 Mountainside, NJ 07092

Book Packaging: Earl Cox & Associates Literary Management
ISBN 10: 1-932450-13-0
ISBN 13: 978-1-932450-13-2
LCCN: 2015960058
Cataloging in Publication Data Available

Printed in the United States of America

First Edition: 2016

This publication is designed to provide accurate and authoritative information in regard to the subject matter covered. It is sold with the understanding that the author and publisher are not engaged in rendering legal, financial or other professional advice.

To all the first-generation, minority, and low-income students out there who want to make college a reality: never give up your college dreams!

Other books by Lynnette Khalfani Cox

College Secrets: How to Save Money, Cut College Costs and Graduate Debt Free

College Secrets for Teens: Money-Saving Ideas for the Pre-College Years

Zero Debt: The Ultimate Guide to Financial Freedom

Zero Debt for College Grads: From Student Loans to Financial Freedom

Perfect Credit: 7 Steps to a Great Credit Rating

Your First Home: The Smart Way to Get It and Keep It

The Money Coach's Guide to Your First Million

Investing Success: How to Conquer 30 Costly Mistakes & Multiply Your Wealth!

The Identity Theft Recovery Guide

Table of Contents

CHAPTER 1

The Truth About Pre-College Summer Programs

One way college-bound students try to get a leg up on the competition — and increase their chances of college admission — is by pursuing academic enrichment activities that go well beyond the typical high school curriculum.

Some students take college-level courses at nearby colleges and universities. Others pursue internships or partake in extracurricular research.

But one of the most popular strategies teens use to increase their college preparedness, and try to look good to admission officers, is enrolling in pre-college programs on various college campuses.

Well, I hate to be the bearer of bad news. But billions of dollars are being spent annually in a fruitless effort to show off the wrong way.

There are nearly 2,000 pre-college programs in America, not to mention plenty of study abroad opportunities and other international programs designed for high school students.

If you partake in these initiatives for the right reasons — and with eyes wide open — they can be enriching, even life-changing experiences. But are these programs likely to get you into the college of your dreams?

In a word: no.

"Attending a Harvard summer program will boost a high school student's chances of admission to Harvard. Right? Wrong!" said Bev Taylor, founder of The Ivy Coach, writing in a no-holds barred article on HuffingtonPost.com. "It's a common misconception, one that way too many parents and high school students buy into year after year. In actuality, it's not so different from little kids believing in the Tooth Fairy," she added.

5 Worst Reasons to Attend a Pre-College Program

Even packagers of pre-college programs — the straight talking ones, that is — readily acknowledge what these programs can and can't be expected to do.

One of those straight talkers is Justin Laman, head of Blueprint Summer Programs, a leading provider of pre-college camps.

Blueprint offers teenagers the opportunity to experience a slice of life at a variety of college campuses, including

George Washington University, Lehigh University, Stonehill College, UCLA, UC San Diego, and the University of Virginia.

Parents and students rave about Blueprint, but Laman candidly admits that these programs aren't for every teen.

In fact, he outlines the 5 *worst* motivations for attending a pre-college program:

1. Because you think attending the program will help you get into that college.

"Don't be fooled by fancy literature and promises that can't be kept! The way you get into college is through grades, classes, essays and test scores — not a pre-college program," Laman says. "There is no magic bullet. Pre-college programs are a tool for you to test-drive college, nothing more. If you go into yours with this mindset you'll get the most out of your pre-college experience. Trust us!"

2. Because my parents made me.

"Oh boy. Parents, don't do it. Don't sign them up just because you think it will be good for them. Have a family discussion about what your student wants. Sometimes a better option is a summer job, internship, travel or even just relaxing and being a kid."

Then again, Laman adds this word of caution to students: "Sometimes Mom does know best. (So) be open to the idea and at least consider a pre-college program with an open mind. Maybe they aren't for you, but check them out. They might be cooler than you think!"

3. Because you have nothing else better to do.

"This goes hand-in-hand with number 2 and we're 50/50 on it. If you have nothing better to do but *want* to go to a pre-college program, by all means," Laman suggests. "Just don't get sucked into the idea that you *have* to do one. What's your passion? What do you enjoy doing? Following your passions looks better on college apps than going through the motions."

4. Because you think it will look good on your college resume.

"First of all, we hate the idea that students actually have resumes these days but sometimes the rules change and you still have to play by them," Laman notes. "Unless your pre-college program is hyper-competitive and world renowned, most likely, no one is going to care that you attended. No offense!"

5. Because your boyfriend/girlfriend is going.

Give college a test-drive alone, Laman recommends. "Coming with someone from home is OK, but not someone who you want to spend every second of every day with. College and pre-college programs are a place and time to explore new things and discover new things about yourself too."

None of this is to suggest that students should never take a pre-college program or sign up for a worthwhile summer initiative. On the contrary, research shows that certain pre-college activities, such as taking college-level courses while still in high school, can have real academic and career benefits.

So the goal is to think carefully about these programs and their benefits, explore various alternatives, and then pursue your passions and interests in the most cost-efficient way.

To do this properly, you must first understand all of your options and know the differences between various types of pre-college initiatives.

Above all, it helps to understand the unvarnished truth about pre-college residential programs at many institutions.

A Skeptic's Point of View About Pre-College Programs

Yes, the faculty, staff and administrators want to help educate young minds. And yes, many aspire to provide college-level exposure and a true college experience for teens.

But like many aspects of college, the typical pre-college program is primarily just a business, pure and simple. Call me a skeptic if you like, but it's true.

The over-arching goal of most pre-college programs is to fill empty dorm beds and make money from students who pay tuition. So pre-college summer programs are largely designed to be revenue generators — and really good ones, too.

The sooner you understand that most colleges and universities run pre-college summer programs to generate revenue – not to spot academically talented students to later enroll in school – the sooner you can put certain things in proper perspective and take the right approach in picking a pre-college program.

What kinds of things need to be examined in the right context? For starters, the avalanche of pre-college mail you may have received, and/or the invitations from third-party marketers to attend various pre-college programs need to be taken not with a *grain* of salt, but a heaping dose of it.

Now I realize that you probably felt extra special when those big-name colleges reached out to you (or your child), right? And you may have delighted in finding your mailbox stuffed with fancy nominations to join "exclusive" societies; pre-college brochures promising to expose you to exciting international "opportunities;" or invitations to join very serious-sounding programs in Washington DC and elsewhere.

Well, I'm sure that you really are a great student and all, but make no mistake about what's going on here, why these colleges are contacting you, and how they go about doing it.

The College Recruitment Frenzy

Andrew Ferguson, the author of *Crazy U: One Dad's Crash Course In Getting His Kid Into College,* explains the situation in plain English.

According to Ferguson, colleges buy lists of college bound students — mainly juniors but also now sophomores — from four sources: The College Board (which administers the SAT and which has a Student Descriptive Questionnaire in the PSAT); the ACT Inc. (the main competitor to the SAT); and two for-profit firms (which are in the list-building business and which get their information by mailing millions of questionnaires to high school teachers for distribution to their students). The cost is approximately 30 cents per name, Ferguson notes.

When students take standardized tests, they "give up their address, GPA, ethnicity, academic interests, and extracurricular activities. They estimate family income and disclose whether they expect to request financial aid," Ferguson says.

"Together, these four lists yield a mother lode of data about nearly every college-bound high school student in the United States," he adds.

This list-buying activity actually represents a tiny fraction of what colleges spend in order to put themselves in front of you and get your attention. There's also big dollars spent on catalogues, viewbooks, visits to high schools, and more.

Four-year colleges now spend an average of $2,311 on recruiting every student who enrolls, according to a report by the National Association for College Admission Counseling.

So here's the bottom line: colleges are spending a lot of money for a reason. They want to boost their rankings and they need to boost their yield: that is, the percentage of students enrolled versus the percentage of students they accept each year.

What's more, since most schools don't have enormous endowments, colleges are constantly in revenue-generation mode — yes, even *nonprofit* institutions.

Colleges and universities get money not just from donors, alumni, and students who enroll as freshmen, sophomores, juniors and seniors. They also get dollars from high school students and their families, who represent the next batch of willing consumers of education.

Too Good to Be True?

Peter Van Buskirk, who runs a popular blog called BestCollegeFit.com, put it best, in a blog post entitled "Too Good to be True?":

> "If you are a high school student in grades 9-11, there is a very good chance you have begun to receive unsolicited messages from a range of organizations informing you of your nomination to be included in a special honor society or to attend summer leadership programs.
>
> On the surface, such nominations are intriguing. In fact, what's not to like about them?! The very notion that you have been nominated to receive recognition for your achievements or to take advantage of extraordinary—not to mention seemingly exclusive—life experiences is almost too good to be true. It's good "ego food" and, who knows, maybe your participation will look good on your college applications.

Before you get too excited, let's take a closer look at what is going on with these "nominations."

They are being sent to you by organizations—businesses, to be sure—that seek to capitalize on the eager hopes and, in some cases, insecurities, of young people as they apply to college. The content that is being offered might be valid, but it is rarely as substantive or meaningful as the nomination would suggest.

A leadership week in Washington, D.C. could be a great experience (if you've never been to D.C. before), but it is certainly not exclusive. Doing volunteer work in Costa Rica sounds exotic and could make a difference in the lives of others—did I mention it sounds exotic?! Hmmm. And a listing with an honor society or "who's who" might make you feel good, but don't expect it to garner much attention in the admission process.

You see, the same "nomination" that you might have received was sent to tens of thousands of other students around the country.

How to Evaluate Pre-College "Nominations"

Van Buskirk concludes with some matter-of-fact advice: "The program sponsors' objective is to sign you up," he says. So he offers several tips to consider as you evaluate the "nominations" that are bound to come your way:

1. **Beware of "who's who" distinctions and "honor" societies outside of your school for which you must pay to be recognized.** *You should never have to pay for a credential.* True honors are earned and will rightfully be bestowed upon you.

2. **Commit your time to others because it gives you joy to do so.** Admission officers are wary of volunteer experiences that can be bought. Remember, they are cynics—and the cynic will see vacation where you had hoped they would see volunteerism.

3. **If you are truly interested in doing community service over the summer—or any time, for that matter—look for opportunities to make a difference in your own community.** Participate in a Habitat for Humanity project. Serve meals to the homeless. Become a Big Brother/Big Sister. The hallmark of service is selflessness.

4. **Choose activities that will be truly enriching.** As you contemplate your options for discretionary involvement, do so as though applying to college is not in the picture. Choose those opportunities that will help you learn and grow. Admission officers look

for authenticity in the person and character of the candidates they are considering. Let your choices be a window into the qualities you possess.

5. **Don't subscribe to special academic programs or camps for high school students on college or university campuses in order to help your chances of getting into those schools.** Keep in mind that, first and foremost, these programs are offered because the host institutions have empty beds to fill over the summer. Do the math. If a school can fill the beds with eager high school students over the course of two or three summer sessions, it will have succeeded in bringing thousands of students to its campus—a financial boon to the institution. Will any of those students be assured an advantage in the subsequent admission process? Maybe, but there are no guarantees. If you choose such a program, do so because it has particular meaning to you. Following a prescribed course of activity simply to impress admission committees can otherwise be incredibly limiting.

Given the knowledge you now have, what's the best way to approach your pre-college summer options?

In the next chapter, I'll present a brief overview of what to expect from most pre-college programs. Then I'll explain, step-by-step, exactly how to find the best programs – that you can attend either free of charge or at a very, very steep discount.

Finally, I'll show you some real-life examples of my advice — and how following my recommendations can save you a boatload of cash.

CHAPTER 2

A Primer on Pre-College Summer Programs and Costs

A pre-college program provided right on a college campus is typically offered in two ways: directly from colleges and universities, or by third-party marketers who create these programs in collaboration with host college campuses.

Both offerings are typically summer pre-college programs.

What can you expect at a typical campus-based, pre-college summer program?

It largely depends on the program. Some summer pre-college programs are heavy on academics and studying — to the point where kids earn college credit (usually 3 to 6 credits) for their efforts.

Others focus on social interaction, leisure activities and fostering a sense of responsibility — in order to help teens transition away from home and learn what it's like to live on their own.

But there are a dizzying array of pre-college programs — sometimes called "summer camps" — to suit virtually every interest, ability and family budget, including:

- ACT and SAT Prep Programs
- Art and Music Programs
- Athletic Programs
- Business Programs
- Drama and Theater Programs
- Engineering Programs
- General Interest Programs
- Leadership Programs
- Literature and Writing Programs
- Math and Science Programs
- Special Education Programs
- Study Abroad Programs
- And more!

Regardless of the program's emphasis, however, most pre-college offerings give students a chance to experience the larger campus community, go on local field trips to areas of interest, or simply engage in extra-curricular activities that may or may not dovetail with various academic topics being studied.

Popular pre-college offerings run directly by well-known schools include programs at Brown University, Carnegie Mellon, Cornell University, Emory University,

George Washington University, Johns Hopkins, New York University, and UC Berkeley, to name a few.

Some of the better-known, third-party packagers of pre-college programs are: Blueprint; Education Unlimited; Explo; Julian Krinsky Camps & Programs; LEADership, Education and Development Program (formerly LEAD Program), Summer Discovery, Summer Fuel and Summer Study, to name a few.

Get Ready for Sticker Shock

Prices for pre-college programs run the gamut, from extremely low cost to outrageously expensive.

To be more specific, some pre-college offerings are free; they cost students and parents no money at all.

Others range from low-cost (anywhere from $50 up to $500 a week) to moderately priced (around $500 to $1,000 weekly) to very expensive (roughly $1,000 to $2,500 or more per week).

Other than price, there is sometimes one less obvious difference between expensive pre-college offerings and their lower-cost or free brethren.

In a nutshell, programs originating directly from most colleges and universities will boast that their faculty leads class sessions and teaches students enrolled in pre-college programs. With third-party programs, that may or may not be the case. Ditto for some free or low-cost programs that sometimes hire outside instructors to do the work.

You will only know for sure by asking questions and carefully reviewing a program's printed materials and online information.

Personally, I wouldn't be overly concerned if my kid enrolled in a pre-college program, whether it was at a prestigious school like Stanford University (on a free, low-cost or full-pay program) or at Alabama's lesser-known *Samford* University (again, via a free, low cost or a full-pay program) — and the instructors were *not* from the campus in question.

As long as the person teaching a pre-college program has the experience, proper academic credentials and background to stand in front of a class and successfully teach, it matters little to me whether he or she went to an "elite" college or currently teaches at one, but it's up to you to decide.

How to Find Your Ideal Pre-College Program

Use the following seven steps and you'll find the right pre-college option, without breaking the bank:

Step #1: Write down what your goal is in attending a pre-college program.

Do you want a residential experience at a specific campus because that college or university is high on your list of target schools?

Are you interested in a pre-college program mainly as a way to test out a possible major or learn more about a subject of interest, such as science, fashion design, architecture or psychology?

Is a certain city or section of the country intriguing to you, or do you yearn to discover whether you'd prefer college life in a big city, small town or a rural environment? Or do you want to attend a pre-college program just to know what it's like to be in a true college setting, and really *any* campus will do?

Whatever your objective, write it down to be clear about your purpose and intent in finding the "right" pre-college program.

Step #2: Identify two to five colleges or universities of interest to you, then go to their websites and create a list of one or two pre-college programs they offer that you'd want to take.

TIPS: Be sure to include at least one local college, but don't just limit your prospects to in-state campuses. (I'll explain why later.) For now, simply cast a wide net. If you have trouble coming up with a list of up to five colleges, don't worry about specific names. Just do an online search of the phrase "pre-college programs" and add some keywords to your search query to narrow your options. For example, if you're curious about an academic pre-college program that might be of interest to art history majors, search "pre-college programs" and "art history." Such a search would lead to you a variety of schools, including the Pratt Institute, Barnard College, and the Maine College of Art.

As part of your online research, find out the exact weekly price of the pre-college programs you've identified.

At this phase, don't let geography, finances or sticker-shock deter you or limit your search options.

If you find a program that truly interests you, put it on your list regardless of cost. Even if the campus is out of town, if the pre-college program is appealing to you and would help you meet your goal, add it as a potential summer program.

NOTE: this list should <u>only</u> include pre-college programs offered *directly* by colleges and universities themselves — not pre-college programs supplied by third-party entities, even if those programs are hosted on your target campus.

Step #3: Go find an alternative, *more affordable* pre-college option at the very same school(s) of interest to you.

Here's where you can add to your list and include pre-college programs run by outside companies or organizations, the firms I refer to as "third-party marketers" of pre-college experiences.

Realize that third-party marketers frequently have cheaper pre-college programs than colleges and universities offer, but that's not always the case. Your job is to locate a *less expensive* option than what the campus is offering directly.

How do you do this? In addition to third-party packagers of pre-college experiences, seek *different routes* into schools of interest: i.e. through minority programs' "pipeline" programs' enrichment opportunities targeting males or females; programs for talented youth; programs that help first-generation college students or teens from low-to-moderate income families; government or community funded pre-college programs, etc. (See examples of these, and a detailed explanation of how to find affordable pre-college programs following the seven steps in this section).

Step #4: Analyze the differences between direct college offerings and third-party programs that are hosted on a college campus.

Be objective in scrutinizing your options. Don't just fall hook, line and sinker for everything you read on a fancy website or in glossy brochures. And don't rule out a campus just because it's not in a certain category, such as being an Ivy League school or an elite, "brand-name" college or university that's well known.

Also, be honest in your evaluation of the differences among the pre-college programs you find.

Does it matter if you were to attend a program and most or all of the other participants were, say, from your own school, town/city or from the same state as you? What if everyone hailed from a different state or a different country than you? Would it bother you if other attendees were predominantly minority or low-income youth?

Would you be uncomfortable interacting with teens from different social, racial, religious, geographic or economic backgrounds? Or would you consider that an opportunity to learn and grow?

Would you care that one program has courses led by college faculty members while another has paid instructors who don't work for the campus?

And what about the structure of the programs? Are you most interested in academic or social activities? Does it have to be a residential offering, where you stay overnight in dorms? Or would you be fine with skipping the immersion experience, and attending a daytime only pre-college program where you commuted back home each day?

Finally, don't forget to evaluate the price differences among pre-college offerings. You can group pre-college programs into four different price categories:

a. Free. These are "no tuition" programs, or sponsored programs where tuition and/or room and board is covered by benefactors, donors, corporations, the college itself, alumni or other parties.

b. Low Cost: Programs that charge about $50 to $500 per week.

c. Moderately Priced: Programs cost roughly $500 to $1,000 weekly.

d. Expensive: Pre-college programs that charge $1,000 to $2,500+ per week.

Step #5: Consider the pros and cons of going with a "local" pre-college program that's actually out of your town or state.

Assume you're from Florida and you want to attend a music-focused pre-college program in Austin, Texas — a city that bills itself as "The Live Music Capital of the

World." The pre-college program you like is called "The Texas Musical Summer Institute" and it appears to only target teens from greater Austin area or the entire Lone Star State (Texas).

Before you dismiss such a program based on the assumptions that it's out of your district or state and it accepts only "local" students, call and ask whether they'd consider taking an out-of-state student. Sometimes slots don't fill up, or the program may welcome the chance to expose its local students to youth from other areas.

Step #6: Inquire about scholarships and tuition discounts at all programs.

Always, always ask about fee reductions, such as full or partial scholarships offered by a pre-college program. You'd be surprised at how many programs simply don't widely advertise the availability of such funds, but there is money to help students nonetheless. Financial support usually comes from the organization itself, non-profits and corporations, as well as patrons who may be alumni or generous benefactors who want to promote college access.

When there is absolutely no money available, a pre-college program will usually say so on its website — typically under the tuition and fees section, or in the FAQ area. If scholarship information isn't found on the site, you stand a good possibility that the program may indeed offer discounts based on:

- Financial need
- Merit and accomplishment
- Personal essays
- Geographic preferences
- Racial, ethnic or socio-economic diversity
- Early enrollment
- Multiple siblings
- Return students
- … and more

So remember to <u>always ask</u> directly about price breaks and tuition discounts, especially if you can't find such info online. The worst that can happen is that they say there are no scholarships or discounts available.

> **TIP:** It's best to start looking for pre-college summer programs during the late fall and early winter seasons. That way you can narrow your list, investigate scholarships if necessary, and be prepared to fill out applications and scholarship forms right around January.

Competitive summer pre-college programs that get a lot of applications (including those for talented youth, and many free offerings) have early deadlines — starting in

December or January and culminating in March or April. Many others' programs, though, have late spring deadlines, rolling deadlines, or some may have deadlines right up until the pre-college program starts or becomes full.

Whatever the case, it's always much safer and wiser to apply *as early as possible*, especially if you're seeking funding. Many pre-college programs provide their scholarships and grants on a "first come, first served" basis, handing out scholarship funds until that money is exhausted.

Step #7: Seek financial aid through college access groups, foundations and educational organizations.

If necessary, take time to seek financial aid through organizations and foundations that offer economic assistance to students who want to enroll in pre-college programs. Some of these resources include:

Achievement First

Bright Futures

Graduation Generation

Jack Kent Cook Foundation

Joyce Ivy Foundation

Minds Matter

QuestBridge

Schuler Scholar Program

Summer Search

Most of these groups require you to submit a scholarship application between January and March in order to receive aid for the summer. So if your goal is to attend a pricey pre-college program, but you can't afford it, I would urge you again to get to work on your funding request early.

If you follow the seven steps I've just outlined, you can definitely find an affordable pre-college program — even many *free* ones — that meet your needs.

Don't believe me? Just keep reading for more truly eye opening and money-saving information.

CHAPTER 3

Finding Free and Low-Cost Pre-College Programs

Have you set your sights exclusively on the popular paid pre-college programs offered directly by well-known colleges and universities across the country? If so, you can expect to shell out big bucks for these pre-college experiences, as I'll now illustrate.

Let's say you have an interest in a business-oriented program. Here's what a half-dozen top schools recently charged for their pre-college summer programs:

Emory University *had a 6-week program, the Emory Institute for Data Science, which paired students with faculty in Economics, and granted 4 college credits.*

Cost: *$9,689 or $1,567 per week.*

Harvard *offered a 7-week program, via its Secondary School Program, with courses like Principles of Economics and International Relations, which granted 8 credits.*

Cost: *$11,000 or $1,571 per week.*

New York University *had a 6-week program, Summer @ Stern, awarding students 8 credits for taking two classes like Business Essentials or Business and Investing.*

Cost: *$11,651 or $1,942 per week.*

Northwestern *had a 6-week College Prep Program that included an Intro to Macroeconomics class and a Marketing Management course, granting students the equivalent of 6 college credits.*

Cost: *$10,000 or $1,667 per week.*

University of Southern California *offered high school students a 4-week course, Exploring Entrepreneurship, which awarded 3 college credits.*

Cost: *$7,416 or $1,854 per week.*

University of Pennsylvania *had a 6-week program that provided students with the equivalent of 6 credits for taking two courses, including Intro to Microeconomics.*

Cost: *$13,299 or $2,217 per week.*

Are you seeing a pricing trend here? At many elite U.S. schools, it's common to spend about $1,500 to $2,000 *weekly* for the privilege of attending residential pre-college programs.

Why are some parents willing to spend small fortunes on these pre-college experiences?

Many are no doubt wealthy parents who feel like they're just paying for the very best education that money can buy. Others may have more shallow motivations. They just want bragging rights, and to be able to say: "My kid is spending the summer at _____ (fill in the blank with a brand-name college or university)."

But for most families, I suspect that they spend all this money due to three factors.

For starters, many parents simply don't know any better. They don't realize that plenty of excellent colleges and universities (including the ones I just listed), actually have *free* summer options and lower-cost pre-college programs, too.

Additionally, too many parents mistakenly think that enrolling their kid in a pre-college program at ultra-selective colleges like Harvard will somehow make that child a shoo-in — or at least give him or her a competitive edge — as a college applicant.

But even Harvard officials, who are no doubt aware of this misconception, try to dispel this myth. On its pre-college website, Harvard notes: "There is no relation between admission to the Harvard Summer School Secondary School Program and admission to the freshman class at Harvard College."

The $2,000 Test Drive

There is a third, and somewhat practical reason, however, that some parents bite the bullet financially and pay for their child to take a pricey pre-college program.

Justin Laman, of Blueprint, sums it up this way: "Some parents would rather make a $2,000 investment now to make sure they don't make a $200,000 mistake down the road."

Laman's point is that it's far cheaper to let a teen "test drive" a college now, rather than find out after several years later that the student is dropping out or wants to change schools because he or she didn't like the college or it wasn't the right fit.

Laman's point is well taken. And I don't blame well-heeled families for making that investment to help their kids really get to know a campus before applying. Nevertheless, for parents who *can't* afford the $2,000 test drive, there is — thankfully — a much better way.

It only requires two things: for you to open your mind to various creative possibilities, and to do your homework.

Free and Low-Cost Summer Options — Even at Ivy League Schools

I've just showed you how expensive it can be to attend some pre-college programs run by top schools.

Now what if I told you that you could attend a pre-college program at some of these same schools, or other prestigious schools, for a fraction of the price — or even no money at all?

It's true. Let's take another look at various pre-college options, this time highlighting a half-dozen *free* pre-college business programs.

Bryant University *runs a pre-college summer business program, known as the PricewaterhouseCoopers Accounting Careers Leadership Institute. Since PWC sponsors the Institute, students pay nothing to participate. Applicants must be African-American or Latino students who are high school juniors (i.e. rising seniors).*

Cost: *$0.*

Indiana University, *Bloomington hosts two different free one-week programs called the Young Women's Institute and MEET Kelley, through the Kelley School of Business. The first program targets females; the latter program is directed toward under-represented minorities, including*

African-American, Latino, Native American and Native Hawaiian/Pacific Islander students.

Cost: *$0.*

North Carolina A&T State University *offers two free, residential programs to high school students, and one free commuter program, called the Agribusiness Institute. The programs are 4 weeks, 1 week and 8 days, respectively, and are offered via the School of Agriculture and Environmental Sciences. Amazingly, some of these programs even offer stipends, essentially paying teenagers for being good students and learning at the campus.*

Cost: *$0.*

Seattle University *provides a weeklong but robust Summer Business Institute via its Albers School of Business and Economics. The program is designed for under-represented students, including African-Americans, Latinos and Native Americans.*

Cost: *$50.*

The Foundation for Teaching Economics *sponsors Economics for Leaders, a free, one-week summer program that takes place on a variety of campuses and is geared toward rising seniors with leadership potential.*

Cost: *$0**

---

*NOTE: While housing, meals and tuition for the program are all free, participants must pay a "program fee" that varies, depending on the campus chosen. In 2014, campus program fees ranged from $600 (at University of Dallas) to $1,400 (at Yale University). Other schools included Vanderbilt ($750), William and Mary ($850), UC Berkeley ($1,000), and Duke University ($1,200), to name a few.

University of Texas at Austin *offers not just one, but two, free weeklong programs sponsored by Ernst & Young through the McCombs School of Business.*

The first program, called McCombs Future Executive Academy (MFEA), lets attendees explore various facets of a business degree and a career in business. The second program, called DYNAMC (Discover Yourself in Accounting Majors and Careers), exposes teens to a broad variety of accounting careers, from working at one of the Big Four global accounting firms to working for the FBI.

All students residing in the U.S. may apply. But the university especially encourages outstanding African-American, Hispanic and Native American students, as well as those who have overcome any social or economic hardship, to apply.

Cost: *$0.*

University of Washington *offers ACAP, or the Accounting Career Awareness Program, a one-week free residency program at the university's Foster School of Business. The program targets minority applicants.*

Cost: *$0.*

Wabash College *provides a free, weeklong program dubbed OLAB, Opportunities to Learn About Business, for rising 12th graders considering a business major. Though Wabash is an all-male liberal arts college, the OLAB program is coed and all students are welcome to apply, regardless of race, gender or intended career choice.*

Cost: *$0.*

I could go on, but you probably get the point: you don't always have to fork over big dollars just to attend a really good pre-college program.

What's the Difference Between Costly Pre-College Programs and Free Ones?

You may have noticed three key differences between the pricey pre-college programs I first mentioned and the latter, free ones.

First, the high-cost programs usually award college credit, whereas the cheaper programs typically don't. That wouldn't be a deal-breaker in my book — not by any stretch of the imagination — especially since you learned earlier in this chapter that the most cost-effective ways to get college credit are through AP testing and CLEP exams. So you don't need a pricey pre-college program just for college credits.

Besides, you can find *free* pre-college programs that offer college credit as well.

Consider **Caldwell College** in New Jersey. It runs Summer College at Caldwell, a free three-week pre-college program for high school juniors to study science, medicine and math. Applicants must be first-generation college students. They earn 3 college credits at no cost because funding for the program comes from the U.S. Department of Education College Access Challenge Grant through the New Jersey Commission on Higher Education.

In New York, all high school students attending public schools can take college-level classes free of charge through College Now, the country's largest dual enrollment and college readiness program. College Now is a growing collaboration between more than 350 New York schools with over 20,000 students and CUNY, the City University of New York. Under most circumstances, when students take courses via College Now, those credits transfer directly within the CUNY system. Similarly, many colleges and universities outside CUNY also accept credits from CUNY campuses.

A second key difference is that the free and/or lower-cost pre-college programs are largely designed to promote racial, ethnic, gender and socio-economic diversity.

And finally, the free, sponsored programs you'll find are typically much shorter in duration, with most spanning one-week or so, instead of 6 weeks.

But does that mean that *all* free pre-college options fall into the category of shorter programs? Absolutely not.

And for those of you thinking: "Great, I'm not a minority, so there are no free options for me," that's not the case at all.

While it's true that the majority of free or subsidized programs are designed to help minorities, economically disadvantaged students or underrepresented youth, it's also the case that pre-college program sponsors recognize the need for diverse students of all backgrounds. They also want to foster college access at many levels.

You may not be a low-income student, and you may not be part of an ethnic or racial minority, but you may possess other unique qualities or special talents and interests that would make you an attractive candidate for pre-college programs.

Additionally, colleges and sponsors with an interest in promoting higher education are keen to help high-ability students who have a passion for learning, but need an expanded platform or more intensive options for learning. As a result, students of all backgrounds can earn acceptance into free pre-college programs. You just have to know where to look, and how to package yourself in the proper way.

Remember: colleges are looking to build a mosaic of students from all walks of life; that's one way they create more vibrant communities and the best possible exchange of ideas and knowledge.

"There's a diversity of perspective and thought that I think schools are looking to create for each of their campuses," says Aramis Gutierrez, who runs a pre-college program at Rutgers University.

Karen Richardson, the Associate Director of Admissions at Tufts University, who is also the school's Director of Diversity Recruitment, agrees.

"When you say the word 'diversity,' most students and parents seem to automatically think about just racial and ethnic diversity," Richardson says. "But we talk about diversity in a very broad sense."

According to Richardson, Tuft's philosophy of building a diverse, inclusive campus means also considering diversity of thought, and a host of other factors, such as socioeconomic status, sexual orientation, religious background, geographic residency and more. The campus even tries to ensure that it has a mix of students that represent diverse types of schools, such as public, private, charter, religious and home-schooled students.

"All of those things are important to make a dynamic campus atmosphere," Richardson says.

Free Pre-College Programs for All Majors and Interests

To further demonstrate my point, let's stop looking at business-focused programs and take a look at programs of interest to students with a variety of academic or professional interests. As you can see, you can find a variety of free and low-to-moderate cost pre-college programs in every state and across every type of campus.

Here are some notable ones to consider, starting with several Ivy League schools:

Harvard offers a free summer 7-week program called the Crimson Summer Academy to local students who attend high schools in Boston or Cambridge.

Princeton University runs a Summer Journalism Program, a no-cost, 10-day program for low-income students that are rising seniors. There's also the tuition-free, multi-year Princeton University Program in Teacher Preparation, called the Princeton University Preparatory Program, or PUPP. It's a rigorous academic program that aids high-achieving, low-income high school students from local districts.

Brown University, another Ivy League school, offers Dean's Scholarships to cover pre-college program costs.

And there are two nifty things about Brown's pre-college programs:

1) They are geared toward students in grades 6 through 12. So even younger students can participate. Parents of middle school kids: start planning early!

2) Brown's pre-college programs also take place in three ways: on campus, online, and abroad, and there are scholarships available for each.

And what about Penn? Remember the hefty price tag for its pre-college program? Well, you could have another very similar pre-college experience at Penn, for far, far less.

Just look into the LEADership, Education and Development Program.

LEAD's Summer Business Institute is for rising seniors who want to attend prestigious campuses like the University of Chicago and University of Pennsylvania. The cost for 4 weeks at Penn via LEAD: it's $2,800, or $700 per week.

Recall that, by comparison, if you went to Penn's website and enrolled in their pre-college program for high school students, the 4-week residential program with two courses for credit would cost you $13,299 (or $10,299 if you only wanted to take one class for credit).

One other word of advice to parents with *younger* children who may have their hearts set on sending their kids to Ivy League colleges or other top schools when they reach college age — It would behoove you to encourage your children to not only be good students during the school year, but to not slack off during the summer.

They certainly never *need* to go to pre-college programs directed towards middle school students, but it's a good idea to keep them active and engaged during the summer — and not in front of the TV all day.

Fortunately (or unfortunately, depending on your perspective), the "pre-college" environment is gradually and continually pushing downward into the lower grades.

The one good thing about this expansion of the definition of what "pre-college" means is that there are more no-cost, academic summer programs than ever before for middle-school students, especially in math and science.

For instance, The ExxonMobil Bernard Harris Summer Science Camp is a free, two-week summer residential program at the New Jersey Institute of Technology that offers activities, experiments, projects, and field experiences for students entering 6th, 7th, or 8th grade in the fall. The camp promotes science, technology, engineering and mathematics (STEM) education and supports historically underserved and underrepresented students with limited opportunities.

For older teens in high school, another terrific — and free — summer science program is The Summer Science Institute (SSI) held at the University of Wisconsin-Madison's Institute for Biology Education. This popular six-week residential experience helps students develop an understanding of biological and physical research. The program also boosts participants' writing and math skills. SSI is open to all students, but minority applicants, first generation students and youth from low-income families are especially encouraged to apply.

Here are a handful of other free and low-cost pre-college programs for minorities, just to give you an inkling of what's available.

Free and Low-Cost Summer Programs for Minorities

Carleton College runs a highly competitive weeklong residential program called the Carleton Liberal Arts Experience in Northfield, MN. The program, only available to the country's top African-American high school students, is totally free. Carleton even pays a student's travel costs to and from the college.

Carnegie Mellon University offers a free and highly regarded 6-week Summer Academy for Minority Students. While this residential science and math program is well known for being intensive, and very competitive to get in, Carnegie Mellon also has a number of other lesser-known but still excellent pre-college programs through its Summer Programs for Diversity. Those other free pre-college options include offerings in Advanced Placement/Early Admission (for college credit); Architecture; Art & Design; Drama; Music; and even a National High School Game Academy exploring the skills needed to be successful in the video gaming industry.

Massachusetts Institute of Technology provides exceptional students with six weeks of tuition-free study at the Minority Introduction to Engineering, Entrepreneurship, and Science program, better known as MITES. MIT also has a much-lauded Research Science Institute, open to students of any background, which likewise has a 6-week no-cost residential program for the next generation of science rock stars. A final one-week residential option is available as well for other talented minority students. Called the Engineering Experience at MIT, it too is offered at no charge.

QuestBridge Summer Program is a highly sought after five or six-week pre-college program with all expenses paid at dozens of top colleges and universities in the country. Students can attend a variety of highly ranked institutions, ranging from Amherst College, University of Chicago, Stanford University and Yale University to Bowdoin College, Columbia University, Vassar College and Wesleyan University. Quest Scholars must be low-income but high-performing students. Even better, successful Quest Scholars are matched with elite institutions that agree to provide full financial aid or a "free ride" to support four years of higher education.

Telluride Association Summer Programs include two programs, known as TASS and TASP, that rank among the country's premier pre-college summer experiences. For six weeks, students study on top-notch campuses, engaging in seminars that explore different themes in the humanities and social sciences. These free summer programs often focus on issues of race and have recently taken place on three campuses: Cornell University, Indiana University and University of Michigan, Ann Arbor. No grades or college credits are given. The programs are designed to simply foster a love of learning and deep scholarly and social inquiry. Telluride targets students from underprivileged and historically underrepresented groups. But TASS and TASP applicants need not be minority students; they only need to demonstrate an interest in African-American studies.

Sewanee: The University of the South recently offered a free two-week program in Asian Studies called FACES, or Freeman Asian Cultural Experiences at Sewanee. Another no-cost program, the Bridge Program in Math and Science at Sewanee, is a three-week residential experience for rising high school seniors of diverse backgrounds. Sewanee is a selective liberal arts college located in rural Tennessee.

Virginia Military Institute offers the College Orientation Workshop (COW), a free, four-week program targeting minority male youth, especially African-Americans, who are rising juniors or seniors in high school.

You may or may not qualify or be interested in any of the programs mentioned in this chapter. But I've already shared a seven-step process for finding quality pre-college programs. So you can use your own research to track down our best options. You should also know of several tricks that can help you along the way. So keep on reading to discover additional ways to cut pre-college program expenses during your high school years.

CHAPTER 4

Strategies to Slash Pre-College Program Expenses

There are plenty of other strategies that students of all backgrounds (and ages) can use to lower their pre-college program costs.

For example, if you just want to learn a subject and don't necessarily require the overnight immersion experience, why not consider a daytime only pre-college option? These are often referred to as "commuter" or "non-residential" programs.

There are plenty of excellent commuter programs, even at top schools, that aren't in the typical $1,500 to $2,000 a week range. In fact, these classes-only alternatives are priced at a fraction of the cost of their residential program counterparts.

At the **University of Virginia**, a non-residential pre-college course of study involving two summer classes for 6 credits cost $2,358 over a six-week period. That works out to about $667 per week. Not cheap, but certainly not overly expensive, either.

It's also a lot less than what UVA charged for a new, 4-week residential program it launched in 2014, called UVA Advance, which also included two classes for six credits, along with room and board, workshops and field trips. Inaugural program fees for UVA Advance were $4,888, or $1,222 weekly for Virginia residents — not to mention twice the cost ($9,999 or $2,500 a week) for non-Virginians.

Commuter Programs Save Big Bucks

Elsewhere in Virginia, **The College of William and Mary** also offered a residential pre-college option, a 3-week program in Early American History that granted 4 credits and likewise included field trips to historic sites. The cost: $3,950 or $1,317 weekly for residents — and $4,150 or $1,383 weekly — for non-residents.

But a high school teen who received permission to take one summer class at William and Mary (without the residential portion), and received the same 4 credits, would have paid just $1,380 for a 5-week American History course, or $276 a week.

Then there's the University of North Carolina at Chapel Hill, which offered 6-week summer courses (5.5 weeks to be exact) to in-state commuters for just $690 apiece. Students taking one class earned 3 units. The cost worked out to just

$115 per week. Adding on-campus housing into the mix, however, tacked on another $846. So opting to commute was a big money-saver.

Overall, most students can save 50% to 80% off a pre-college program by taking the commuter option, instead of choosing the residential program experience.

Consider Lesser-Known Colleges To Cut Pre-College Costs

Another tactic when you simply want to learn about a subject or get exposure to a topic, is to target schools *away* from large cities, and consider campuses that aren't necessarily "brand name" institutions. Many colleges and universities outside of major metro areas — along with suburban, rural or just lesser-known campuses — often run outstanding pre-collegiate programs.

One terrific pre-college program is the Summer Honors Program at Indiana University of Pennsylvania. Hosted by IUP's Cook Honors College, the program gives students a chance to study whatever they're interested in — from archaeology, biochemistry, and from law to film and television, journalism or East Asian culture. And thanks to a generous alumni base, the college is able to offer $1,000 scholarships to all attendees, bringing down the cost of this 2-week residential program to just $300 — or $150 a week.

Elon Academy, at Elon University in North Carolina, is another stellar pre-college program and it's free of charge. Originally launched and funded by Elon itself, the Academy is now supported by the generosity of businesses, foundations and individuals.

Elon Academy serves promising local high school students who have financial need or no family history of college. Recent scholars at Elon Academy have spent their summers studying criminal justice, creating writing, philosophy, engineering, ancient philosophy and more. The program's multi-year summer residential experiences are rounded out with year-round Saturday programs for students and their families. In recent years, three Elon Academy participants have won the prestigious and coveted Gates Millennium Scholarship, covering all college expenses.

Get Pre-College Funding Help From Uncle Sam

Another strategy for finding free and low-cost pre-colleges: go with a government or quasi-government sponsored program, one that is funded by state or federal resources. Examples include:

CDC Disease Detective Camp

This is a free, weeklong commuter program sponsored by the David J. Sencer CDC Museum in association with the Smithsonian Institution. The focus of the CDC Disease Detective Camp is public health and the science of epidemiology. (For middle school students, there is also a separate Junior CDC Disease Detective Camp that runs for three days and is likewise free of charge.) The camps are held at CDC headquarters in Atlanta and are open to all U.S. high school juniors and seniors at least 16 years old.

GEAR UP

GEAR UP is a federally funded program that prepares students for college success. GEAR UP stands for Gaining Early Awareness and Readiness for Undergraduate Programs.

These free offerings can be found at scores of good campuses across America, such as **Texas A&M University**, which provides GEAR UP "College Ready Camps" for local youth who aspire to achieve a higher education.

The National Council for Community and Education Partnerships maintains a Web-based GEAR UP Program Locator.

Governor's Schools

Governor's Schools are special summer programs for gifted students that are fully or partially funded by state legislatures and/or governor's offices. As a result, most are free; but some do have modest tuition charges.

In order to attend a governor's school you must be a resident of a state that offers this program. There are currently about two-dozen U.S. states with Governor's Schools, including Alabama, California, Florida, Georgia, New Jersey, New York, North Carolina, Pennsylvania, and Virginia.

These programs are typically residential in nature; but some are commuter programs. Also, while governor's schools vary by state, they are usually hosted on college or university campuses, giving high-achieving teens the chance to develop intellectually and socially.

The National Conference of Governor's Schools is the national organization of summer residential governor's school programs. At their website you can find links to Governor's School Programs by state.

NSLI-Y

The National Security Language Initiative for Youth, or NSLI-Y, is a free study abroad program for high school students sponsored by the U.S. State Department. The goal is to teach students one of seven lesser-known languages: Chinese (Mandarin), Hindi, Arabic, Russian, Korean, Turkish, and Persian (Tajik).

The NSLI-Y pre-college option is a not only residential program; it's also an intensive language immersion experience in a variety of locations around the world. And best of all: because it's backed by a federal agency, it's free for students accepted into this highly selective program.

TriO Programs

TriO programs are federally backed educational opportunity outreach programs designed to assist students from disadvantaged backgrounds. There are eight TriO programs in the United States, including three directly targeting elementary, middle-school and high-school aged youth:

- Educational Talent Search
- Upward Bound
- Upward Bound Math-Science

These programs vary in length and structure, but many offer no-cost, multi-week residential programs for pre-college students at colleges and universities across the country. They also include additional academic instruction, tutoring and ongoing educational support services throughout the school year.

For example, the Upward Bound Program at the **University of Maryland** has two parts: a six-week residential summer session (with classes in math, science, composition, foreign language and more), as well as year-round academic sessions to complement summer activities.

In general, to qualify for an Upward Bound or Talent Search program, a student must meet the federal guideline for "low income" or must be a "first-generation student" who is college bound. The definition of "first generation student" means the parent(s) living in a student's household does/do not have a Bachelor's degree.

The National College Access Network has an online program directory that lists college access programs (including TriO programs) by state.

Even if you don't go to a TriO program or qualify as low-income, remember this point: high school students can attend pre-college summer programs like the others described above – and you can do it 100% free, courtesy of the U.S. government.

More Pre-College Search Tips

If you ever face difficulty finding pre-college programs, there are several good online resources to help you track down the right one. These online sites include:

- http://www.enrichmentalley.com
- http://www.studenteducationprograms.com
- http://www.Usummer.com

And if the program you want to attend doesn't offer full scholarships or deep discounts, don't neglect to seek other funding sources. Check with your local PTA, religious organizations and faith-based groups, as well as civic associations, such as Alumni Associations, Kiwanis, Lions, Rotary, and more.

Local, regional and national organizations devoted to promoting college access can also be a wealth of information — and a fantastic source for funding as well. These groups often have dollars to make your pre-college program dreams a reality, or if they don't offer scholarship dollars directly, they can point you in the right direction for funding.

For example, at the regional level, Our Next Generation offers scholarships to students in the greater Milwaukee area to help support their attendance in pre-college programs:

Street Squash provides scholarships for summer camps and pre-college programs to youth in Harlem and Newark.

And the Assistance League of Seattle has an "Enrichment Scholarship Program" that provides scholarships for summer programs available to Seattle Public School children, grades

6 to 11. Students can pursue activities and academics in numerous fields such as music, art, science, mathematics, language, drama, technology, leadership, and outdoor experiences.

So be sure to do an online search of phrases like: "pre-college scholarship application" or "pre-college tuition scholarship" along with the name of the city or state in which you live.

Time Invested = Dollars Saved

Is all this too much work to do? No, not in the slightest — especially for the payoff your efforts will generate.

I'm asking you to make an investment in yourself, an investment of time that will save you and your family thousands and thousands of dollars. Isn't a few hours, or even a few days' worth of research and information gathering worth that?

How I Saved More than $4,000 on My Kids' Pre-College Programs

For example, when my oldest daughter expressed an interest in going to a pre-college program at my alma mater, the University of Southern California, I gladly obliged. Her goals were three-fold: to check out USC and see if she liked the campus, to determine if she'd be OK living so far away from home, and also to boost her public speaking skills.

I could have signed her up for the shortest program offered directly from USC. That was a two-week residential program that cost about $3,500.

But I knew there had to be more affordable options.

Sure enough, we found a local program, called the California Youth Think Tank (CYTT). It offered a one-week leadership program at USC designed to help students prepare for college and career success, and get to know USC's campus. Just like USC's program, students of CYTT enjoyed stimulating classes and activities, got official USC student ID cards and stayed for a week in USC dormitories.

On the surface, CYTT appeared to be only for students of the Golden State. But when I called the Program Director, William Young, who has run CYTT for more than two decades, he told me he would welcome an application from a New Jersey student.

My daughter applied, got in, and had a wonderful experience, which included making public presentations and participating in a student debate team during the program.

The price? Less than $500, a small fraction of the cost our family would have paid by going directly through USC. Money saved: $3,000.

Another time, when researching summer programs for my son, who is an outdoor enthusiast and loves the wilderness, I discovered a real low-cost gem: 4H Youth Development Programs.

In my region, the Lindley G. Cook 4-H Youth Center for Outdoor Education, is a low-to-moderate cost outdoor education camp operated by Rutgers Cooperative Extension of Rutgers University. Participants are not required to be 4H members.

During the most recent summer, a weeklong camp program was just $550, with $50 discounts for many attendees, including early bird registrants, 4H members, military members, and Rutgers employees, as well as those with siblings enrolled.

But I actually found an even lower-cost option for my outdoor loving son: a weeklong program run by a non-profit called The Children of the Earth Foundation. I barely believed my eyes when I saw online that they were offering a special price of just $100 for a 6-day program for teens interested in a "survival camp." (The normal price was originally $695 for the week).

At Children of the Earth, youth, teens and families learn the ancient art and science of tracking, awareness, and wilderness living skills. Not only did my 14-year-old jump at the chance to attend, but my husband and I gladly drove our son the nearly two hours it took to get from our home in New Jersey to the multi-acre campsite in Holmes, New York.

After making his own survival shelter from materials in the forest and staying in it overnight, finding and purifying water in the woods, creating fire from nature and learning how to identify more than a half dozen wild, edible plants, my teenager grew up so much and came home completely enchanted by the entire experience. "It was amazing," my son told me.

Then he pleaded with us to let him attend the camp for *another* week. His father and I agreed. So I dropped my son off at camp again, where he learned even more, including how to track animals and humans based on prints left on the ground. Again, all of this cost a mere $100 a week.

Mind you, I was initially prepared to spend $550 a week at 4H or to at least *consider* the $695 weekly cost at Children of the Earth. Then the $100 a week offer made it a no-brainer. Total cash saved: about $1,200.

So make no mistake about it: both free and low cost pre-college programs of all kinds do exist. And some of them are truly life changing.

Do the Program Shuffle

Here's yet another creative way to find a cost-effective pre-college program when you hope to be at a specific college or university but are undecided about a major or a career choice. I call this method "the Program Shuffle."

In a nutshell, it involves taking a look at *all* the various pre-college offerings a campus provides — not just the ones the college or university showcases on the home page of its pre-college program website. Sometimes, the price difference among programs is shocking.

Notre Dame's pre-college programs are a perfect example.

Here's what students and their families were asked to pay for various pre-college programs, all taking place at Notre Dame in the summer of 2014.

If you went online to Notre Dame's Office of Pre-College Programs, you would have found two wonderful programs prominently featured on the site's home page:

The Notre Dame Leadership Seminars were 11-day residential programs sponsored by the college and offered free of charge to talented, rising high school seniors. Notre Dame even paid the students' transportation costs to and from the campus, and granted students one college credit.

By comparison, Notre Dame's Summer Scholars Program was a two-week residential offering that provided one college credit, and cost $3,100.

Both programs offered exceptional learning opportunities and were competitive. But one was sponsored free, while the other required tuition and fees.

What about other pre-college offerings from this distinguished school? Actually, there were plenty of other options, varying in cost and focus.

Notre Dame's PAN (Physics of Atomic Nuclei) Program is a free weeklong residential summer camp for high school students, which takes place at the Nuclear Science Laboratory (NSL) at Notre Dame. The program is run by the Joint Institute for Nuclear Astrophysics (JINA) and NSL.

Notre Dame's Vision Program for students who want to learn about God's role in their lives is a five-day residential program that cost $450 or $475, depending on how early you submitted your application.

Notre Dame's Intro to Engineering Program is a two-week residential program for rising seniors that cost $1,850.

Notre Dame's Career Discovery for High School Students is a 13-day residential study initiative focused on architecture that cost $1,900.

And Notre Dame's International Leadership, Enrichment and Development Program is a 15-day program that cost $3,500.

So if you're not totally wed to pursuing one particular course of study, but you are very interested in a specific campus, do you see how doing the "program shuffle" — that is, being open to various programs and weighing all your options — could be a big money saver?

In fact, students can sometimes cut their pre-college program expenses in half, just by being flexible about which summer option they choose at a given college.

What's more, this tactic can pay off in other ways.

By being open-minded and creative in your approach to pre-college programs, you may push your intellectual, physical and social boundaries, deepen your love of a particular area, or even explore a new field and find it incredibly fascinating.

And isn't that what college is all about?

The Benefits of Leveraging Professional Associations

A final smart way to locate pre-college programs of interest, and secure funding to attend one, is to go through professional associations.

Such searches can be very fruitful.

For example, let's say you're interested in journalism. You might discover JCamp, a six-day residential journalism program offered by the Asian American Journalists Association, which is free of charge to rising high school sophomores, juniors and seniors. (And no, you don't have to be Asian to qualify. There's no requirement to be an AAJA member either).

Those interested in medicine might consult the website of the Association of American Medical Colleges, which has a database list of summer programs in the medical field. This database resource helps students of all ages — from elementary students to undergraduates and graduate students — to locate enrichment programs on medical school campuses.

Another case in point: the American Mathematical Society maintains a list of summer programs, including several free and low-cost math camps.

Why are professional associations and career-related membership groups great places to find pre-college programs, especially affordable ones?

It's because they have a vested interested in students. They know the hurdles students will face academically, financially, socially and professionally. They've been there. And they want to help train and guide the next generation of future leaders in their respective industries. Many also want to give back simply because it's the right thing to do, or because they're grateful for their own success and the opportunities they've been afforded.

Some professional groups take a particular interest in supporting minorities, economically disadvantaged youth and under-represented students. They know the demographics of our society are changing. They realize that we are becoming an increasingly multi-cultural and global society. So these professional, industry and trade groups believe it is in the public's best interest to find and utilize all of our collective resources — human, financial, intellectual and otherwise — in order to prepare for the challenges of the next century.

Within these professional groups, as well as many undergraduate and graduate school programs, you can find "pipeline" programs that specifically target diverse students. These can be goldmines of opportunity for youth that possess academic and professional promise — along with the necessary passion, creativity, and initiative to help them stand out from the crowd.

CHAPTER 5

How to Properly Capitalize on Pre-College Programs

would be remiss in my duties if I merely ended this guidebook here. So many people will urge you to attend a pre-college program as if simply listing the program on a resume were a magic passport of some kind, granting you easy access to the college or future of your dreams.

Obviously, that simply isn't true.

So let's talk about what is perhaps one of the most critical aspects of the pre-college program: what you do *during* and *after* the program ends.

The students who are most successful in capitalizing on pre-college experiences are those that do three things:

- Connect
- Contribute
- Communicate

Here's what each of these ideas entails, and how you can utilize each strategy to your benefit.

The Power of Making Personal Connections

We've all heard the expression: "it's not *what* you know, but *who* you know." It's a saying that basically means your personal connections are more important than your knowledge and skill set. The Chinese word for this concept is "guanxi" — which generally refers to one's personal relationships and other networks of influence.

I'll admit that I have mixed feelings about this concept.

At this point in my adult life, I'm wise enough to know that many people do indeed get ahead — or at least get a shot at their dreams — simply because of a personal or professional contact who pulled some strings, put in a good word, or just opened the right door.

Is this right? Is this fair? I'll leave that up to you to decide. But I think we all agree that it's reality. Even if you don't subscribe wholeheartedly to the belief that "it's *who* you know" that matters most, you probably can at least acknowledge that relationships do matter.

I also know from personal and professional experience, that "getting ahead" also requires hard work, talent — and knowledge. So it's not like you can completely skip the whole business of learning and acquiring skills, and purely rely on "*who* you know."

Given this reality — that it's beneficial to know your stuff *and* to know the "right" people — how should you utilize your time during a pre-college program?

I suggest that in addition to learning, taking the field trips, socializing and so on, that you take some time to strategically connect with key individuals.

Which individuals you choose to connect with really depends on your personal interests, goals and priorities.

Getting to Know the 'Right' People

For example, assume you hope to be a recruited athlete in football, but you're actually going to an academic pre-college program in Forensic Science because you love the whole CSI (Crime Scene Investigation) thing, and you're focused on that or criminal justice as a college major.

Well, naturally, you want to hit the books, study hard, and learn everything you can about forensic science during your pre-college program.

But also carve out some time during that stint to meet the head of the department, to personally introduce yourself to a professor whose work you've read about or whose dissertation or book you've read. You might also spend some time during office hours with a key researcher in the program simply learning about his or her background and what put that person on his or her career path.

By connecting with these people, you'll not only learn a lot more, you'll also make an impression on them and be more memorable than the countless mass of teens passing through these programs month after month and summer after summer.

And what about your sports interest? Don't you dare leave that campus without going to meet the football coach, talking to current players, and getting a more up-close and personal view of the football program. That will be far more insightful than simply taking a group tour, reading a brochure, or perusing information on the campus' website.

So in summary, you want to connect with key faculty, staff, coaches, students and any other individuals that may share an interest with you. These people may be tenured or adjunct professors, guest lecturers, outside speakers, admissions officials, financial aid personnel, department heads, student outreach officers, current freshmen, sophomores, juniors or seniors on campus, as well as other participants in the pre-college program, and more.

You never know how such relationships could develop down the road.

Needless to say, I'm not suggesting that you turn into a networking maniac and feel the need to "work the room" wherever you go. Just be yourself and try to make natural conversation with people (even if you're shy!) — and that's a really good start.

Why Students Must Contribute to the Program

While enrolled in a summer program, it's important to make a meaningful contribution.

What do you have to contribute? You can contribute in many ways: you can contribute to the larger campus, to the ongoing conversations in your group, and to the culture of the program.

The point is: Don't be a wallflower. Be assertive. Get in there, mix it up, and take advantage of opportunities presented to you, as well as the opportunities that arise to make an impact by sharing your time and talents. At the same time, stretch your boundaries and be willing to try new things. Don't be afraid to also share your personal story, your academic experiences, as well as inform people about your background or what drives and motivates you.

You probably do some of this already during the academic year. You may be contributing to your local community, to your school, or to various clubs in a host of ways. So figure out a way to make an impact on other participants in your pre-college program too.

Helping, Leading and Providing Constructive Feedback

One way to contribute is simply by being helpful. Perhaps you know a shortcut, a trick or a better way of doing something that others do not. Or maybe you notice another participant struggling to do or understand something, and you have the skills and the willingness to help that other person.

You may also help your cohorts by taking on a leadership role during group projects, study sessions, research, field activities or other pre-college program work.

In any group, there are many interpersonal and work dynamics. Sometimes, those with outgoing personalities or very strong verbal skills seem to naturally rise to the occasion, taking on leadership roles or becoming official or unofficial group leaders.

Even if you don't consider yourself a natural-born leader, or an assertive, "take-charge" kind of person, that shouldn't stop you from making a contribution. Your thoughts and ideas, your unique approach, your problem-solving skills and your input all matter. So no matter what your personality type, don't hesitate to pipe up and be heard.

You're in that pre-college program for a reason. Someone has already recognized that you belong there. So take advantage of all that the program has to offer — including an environment that fosters intellectual and social engagement. That's one key way you can make a contribution.

Even providing feedback to program directors and coordinators can be a way of making a meaningful contribution.

There's nothing to stop you from offering a program director some good ideas — some might say constructive criticism — to let him or her know what they could do to improve an offering.

It could be something as simple as recommending a course element that would be great to add or an excursion that could be improved in a certain way. Or perhaps you could offer your feedback on how to improve the program's mix of experiential learning (i.e. doing stuff) with the academic learning (via books, lectures, seminars and so on).

Pre-college officials and your peers will likely appreciate your input. Making suggestions for program improvements requires tact, of course. Don't bash any program or sound ungrateful for the opportunity to be there. Just approach it graciously, and say something like: "This has been a really rewarding program, and I have an idea I'd like to share on how to make it even better."

The Essential Final Ingredient: Communication

The final step in making your pre-college program experience a true success is in communicating with others after the program ends.

Ideally, your communication will come in verbal and written form.

For starters, do send a thank you note to the program head, letting him or her know that you appreciated the time spent there.

You can also share what you learned and what you gained from the experience.

And remember all those people you met during the program as well? Now is the time to follow-up with them. Do it soon after you return home, while the memories are still fresh in your mind.

Very often, when teens meet others students (and adults) during pre-college programs, they promise to keep in touch

— but then everyone gets busy and life gets in the way. So the individuals you reach out to will appreciate your diligence and follow-through.

Perhaps most importantly, however, you need to be able to convey to others — people who weren't at your pre-college program — how the experience benefited you.

Let's say you have a college interview. If an admissions officer or a college alum asks you about your pre-college program, you should be able to clearly articulate the importance of the experience and explain how it helped to prepare you for college, expand your knowledge about something, or maybe brought new revelations.

Doing this effectively will require some reflection on your part. It's not simply enough to run down a laundry list of pre-college program activities. The important thing to explain is: what were your personal takeaways from those activities? How did the program help you to learn and grow?

For those who are into journaling (and even those who aren't), writing down your day's activities, academic or personal lessons learned, and other insights as they come to you, preferably while you're enrolled in the program, will be helpful in later remembering the breadth of your pre-college experience.

But since there's often little to no down-time during many pre-college programs, even just jotting down a few notes about special highlights is advisable each day or every few days. You can also do this after the fact, if you absolutely can't squeeze it in during the program.

It's also possible that you may later use some of those notes to explain — in a college essay or a scholarship application — some key part of your pre-college experience.

Again, communication about your pre-collegiate event is a critically important component of the entire experience. So be careful not to neglect this vital aspect.

By now you have a really good sense of the breadth of opportunities available to you in the realm of pre-college programs. And hopefully, you also fully understand that you don't have to go broke trying to pay for these pre-collegiate experiences.

Good luck in your hunt for pre-college programs and in your quest to prepare for college or the workforce once you graduate from high school!

Lightning Source UK Ltd.
Milton Keynes UK
UKOW05f1128100417
298775UK00001B/31/P